family favourites
chicken

Bath · New York · Singapore · Hong Kong · Cologne · Delhi · Melbourne

chicken, cheese & rocket salad

ingredients

SERVES 4

150 g/5$\frac{1}{2}$ oz rocket leaves

2 celery stalks, trimmed
   and sliced

$\frac{1}{2}$ cucumber, sliced

2 spring onions, trimmed
   and sliced

2 tbsp chopped
   fresh parsley

25 g/1 oz walnut pieces

350 g/12 oz boneless roast
   chicken, sliced

125 g/4$\frac{1}{2}$ oz Stilton cheese,
   cubed

handful of seedless
   red grapes, cut in
   half (optional)

salt and pepper

dressing

2 tbsp olive oil

1 tbsp sherry vinegar

1 tsp Dijon mustard

1 tbsp chopped
   mixed herbs

method

1 Wash the rocket leaves, pat dry with kitchen paper and put them into a large salad bowl. Add the celery, cucumber, spring onions, parsley and walnuts and mix together well. Transfer onto a large serving platter. Arrange the chicken slices over the salad, then scatter over the cheese. Add the red grapes, if using. Season well with salt and pepper.

2 To make the dressing, put all the ingredients into a screw-top jar and shake well. Alternatively, put them into a bowl and mix together well. Drizzle the dressing over the salad and serve.

red chicken salad

ingredients

SERVES 4

4 boneless chicken breasts

2 tbsp red curry paste

2 tbsp vegetable or peanut oil

1 head Napa cabbage,
    shredded

175 g/6 oz pak choi, torn into
    large pieces

$1/2$ savoy cabbage, shredded

2 shallots, chopped finely

2 garlic cloves, crushed

1 tbsp rice wine vinegar

2 tbsp sweet chilli sauce

2 tbsp Thai soy sauce

method

1 Slash the flesh of the chicken several times and rub the curry paste into each cut. Cover and chill overnight.

2 Cook in a heavy-based saucepan over medium heat or on a griddle pan for 5–6 minutes, turning once or twice, until cooked through. Keep warm.

3 Heat 1 tablespoon of the oil in a wok or large frying pan and stir-fry the Napa cabbage, pak choi and savoy cabbage until just wilted. Add the remaining oil, shallots and garlic and stir-fry until just tender, but not browned. Add the vinegar, chilli sauce and soy. Remove from the heat.

4 Arrange the leaves on 4 serving plates. Slice the chicken, arrange on the salad greens and drizzle the hot dressing over. Serve immediately.

thai chicken salad

ingredients

SERVES 6

vegetable oil spray

115 g/4 oz skinless chicken
    breast, cut lengthways
    horizontally

3 limes

dressing

1 tbsp finely shredded lemon
    grass

1 small green chilli, finely
    chopped

3 tbsp lime juice

1-cm/$1/2$-inch galangal or root
    ginger, peeled and thinly
    sliced into strips

$1^1/_2$ tsp sugar

2 tbsp white wine vinegar

3 fl oz water

$1^1/_2$ tsp cornflour

salad

25 g/1 oz rice vermicelli

50 g/$1^3/_4$ oz mixed peppers,
    deseeded

50 g/$1^3/_4$ oz carrot

50 g/$1^3/_4$ oz courgette

50 g/$1^3/_4$ oz mangetout

50 g/$1^3/_4$ oz baby corn

50 g/$1^3/_4$ oz broccoli florets

50 g/$1^3/_4$ oz pak choi

4 tbsp roughly chopped fresh
    coriander leaves

method

1 To make the dressing, put all the dressing ingredients, except the cornflour, into a small saucepan over low heat and bring to the boil. Blend the cornflour with a little cold water, gradually add to the pan, stirring constantly, and cook until thickened. Remove from the heat and let cool.

2 Heat a griddle pan over high heat and spray lightly with oil. Add the chicken and cook for 2 minutes on each side, or until thoroughly cooked through. Remove the chicken from the pan and shred.

3 To make the salad, cover the rice vermicelli with boiling water then let it cool in the water. Meanwhile, finely slice the peppers, carrot, courgette, mangetout and baby corn into strips. Cut the broccoli florets into 5-mm/$1/4$-inch pieces and shred the pak choi. Drain the rice vermicelli and put all the salad ingredients with the chicken into a large bowl. Pour over the dressing and toss together, making sure that all the ingredients are well coated.

4 Cover and refrigerate for at least 2 hours before serving. Serve with the juice from half a lime squeezed over each portion.

chicken in lemon & garlic

ingredients

SERVES 6–8

4 large skinless, boneless
   chicken breasts
5 tbsp Spanish olive oil
1 onion, finely chopped
6 garlic cloves,
   finely chopped
grated rind of 1 lemon, finely
   pared rind of 1 lemon and
   juice of both lemons
4 tbsp chopped fresh
   flat-leaf parsley, plus extra
   to garnish
salt and pepper
lemon wedges and crusty
   bread, to serve

method

1 Using a sharp knife, slice the chicken breasts widthways into very thin slices. Heat the olive oil in a large, heavy-based frying pan, add the onion and cook for 5 minutes, or until softened, but not browned. Add the garlic and cook for a further 30 seconds.

2 Add the sliced chicken to the pan and cook gently for 5–10 minutes, stirring from time to time, until all the ingredients are lightly browned and the chicken is tender.

3 Add the grated lemon rind and the lemon juice and let it bubble. At the same time, deglaze the pan by scraping and stirring all the bits on the bottom of the pan into the juices with a wooden spoon. Remove the skillet from the heat, stir in the parsley and season with salt and pepper.

4 Transfer, piping hot, to a warmed serving dish. Sprinkle with the pared lemon rind, garnish with the parsley and serve with lemon wedges for squeezing over the chicken, accompanied by chunks or slices of crusty bread for mopping up the juices.

soy chicken wings

ingredients

SERVES 3–4

250 g/9 oz chicken wings,
    defrosted if frozen

250 ml/8 fl oz water

1 tbsp sliced spring onion

2.5-cm/1-inch piece of fresh
    root ginger, cut into
    4 slices

2 tbsp light soy sauce

1/2 tsp dark soy sauce

1 star anise

1 tsp sugar

method

1 Wash and dry the chicken wings. In a small saucepan, bring the water to the boil, then add the chicken, spring onion and ginger and bring back to the boil.

2 Add the remaining ingredients, then cover and simmer for 30 minutes.

3 Using a slotted spoon, remove the chicken wings from any remaining liquid and serve hot.

five-spice chicken with vegetables

ingredients

SERVES 4

2 tbsp sesame oil

1 garlic clove, chopped

3 spring onions, trimmed
    and sliced

1 tbsp cornflour

2 tbsp rice wine

4 skinless chicken breasts,
    cut into strips

1 tbsp Chinese
    five-spice powder

1 tbsp grated fresh root
    ginger

125 ml/4 fl oz chicken stock

100 g/3½ oz baby corn cobs,
    sliced

300 g/10½ oz beansprouts

finely chopped spring onions,
    to garnish, optional

freshly cooked jasmine rice,
    to serve

method

1 Heat the oil in a preheated wok or large frying pan. Add the garlic and spring onions and stir-fry over medium–high heat for 1 minute.

2 In a bowl, mix together the cornflour and rice wine, then add the mixture to the pan. Stir-fry for 1 minute, then add the chicken, five-spice powder, ginger and chicken stock and cook for another 4 minutes. Add the corn cobs and cook for 2 minutes, then add the beansprouts and cook for another minute.

3 Remove from the heat, garnish with chopped spring onions, if using, and serve with freshly cooked jasmine rice.

chicken satay

ingredients

SERVES 4

2 tbsp vegetable or peanut oil

1 tbsp sesame oil

juice of $1/2$ lime

2 skinless, boneless chicken
   breasts, cut into small cubes

dip

2 tbsp vegetable or peanut oil

1 small onion, chopped finely

1 small fresh green chilli,
   deseeded and chopped

1 garlic clove, chopped finely

115 g/4 oz crunchy peanut
   butter

6–8 tbsp water

juice of $1/2$ lime

method

1 Combine both the oils and the lime juice in a non-metallic dish. Add the chicken cubes, cover with clingfilm and chill for 1 hour. Soak 8–12 wooden skewers in cold water for 30 minutes before use, to prevent burning.

2 To make the dip, heat the oil in a frying pan and sauté the onion, chilli and garlic over low heat, stirring occasionally, for about 5 minutes, until just softened. Add the peanut butter, water and lime juice and simmer gently, stirring constantly, until the peanut butter has softened enough to make a dip – you may need to add a little extra water to make a thinner consistency.

3 Meanwhile, drain the chicken cubes and thread them onto the wooden skewers. Put under a hot grill or on a barbecue, turning frequently, for about 10 minutes, until cooked and browned. Serve hot with the warm dip.

sweet-&-sour chicken

ingredients

SERVES 4–6

450 g/1 lb lean chicken meat, cubed

5 tbsp vegetable or peanut oil

1/2 tsp minced garlic

1/2 tsp finely chopped fresh root ginger

1 green pepper, coarsely chopped

1 onion, coarsely chopped

1 carrot, finely sliced

1 tsp sesame oil

1 tbsp finely chopped spring onion

freshly cooked rice, to serve

marinade

2 tsp light soy sauce

1 tsp Shaoxing rice wine

pinch of white pepper

1/2 tsp salt

dash of sesame oil

sauce

8 tbsp rice vinegar

4 tbsp sugar

2 tsp light soy sauce

6 tbsp tomato ketchup

method

1 Place all the marinade ingredients in a bowl and marinate the chicken pieces for at least 20 minutes.

2 To prepare the sauce, heat the vinegar in a saucepan and add the sugar, light soy sauce and tomato ketchup. Stir to dissolve the sugar, then set aside.

3 In a preheated wok or deep pan, heat 3 tablespoons of the oil and stir-fry the chicken until it starts to turn golden brown. Remove and set aside.

4 In the clean wok or deep saucepan, heat the remaining oil and cook the garlic and ginger until fragrant. Add the vegetables and cook for 2 minutes. Add the chicken and cook for 1 minute. Finally, add the sauce and sesame oil, then stir in the spring onion and serve with rice.

lime chicken with mint

ingredients

SERVES 6

3 tbsp finely chopped
    fresh mint
4 tbsp honey
4 tbsp lime juice
salt and pepper
12 boneless chicken thighs
mixed salad, to serve

sauce

150 ml/5 fl oz low-fat thick
    plain yogurt
1 tbsp finely chopped
    fresh mint
2 tsp finely grated lime rind

method

1 Mix the mint, honey and lime juice in a large bowl and season with salt and pepper. Use cocktail sticks to keep the chicken thighs in neat shapes and add the chicken to the marinade, turning to coat evenly.

2 Cover with clingfilm and marinate the chicken in the refrigerator for at least 30 minutes. Remove the chicken from the marinade and drain. Set aside the marinade.

3 Preheat the grill to medium. Place the chicken on a grill rack and cook under the hot grill for 15–18 minutes, or until the chicken is tender and the juices run clear when the tip of a knife is inserted into the thickest part of the meat, turning the chicken frequently and basting with the marinade.

4 Meanwhile, combine all the sauce ingredients in a bowl. Remove the cocktail sticks and serve the chicken with a mixed salad and the sauce, for dipping.

bacon-wrapped chicken burgers

ingredients

SERVES 4

450 g/1 lb fresh ground
    chicken
1 onion, grated
2 garlic cloves, crushed
55 g/2 oz pine nuts, toasted
55 g/2 oz Gruyère cheese,
    grated
2 tbsp fresh snipped chives
salt and pepper
2 tbsp wholewheat flour
8 lean Canadian bacon slices
1–2 tbsp corn oil
crusty rolls, chopped lettuce
    and red onion rings,
    to serve
mayonnaise and chopped
    spring onions (green part
    only), to garnish

method

1 Place the ground chicken, onion, garlic, pine nuts, cheese, chives and salt and pepper in a food processor. Using the pulse button, blend the mixture together using short sharp bursts. Scrape out onto a board and shape into 4 even-size burgers. Coat in the flour, then cover and chill for 1 hour.

2 Wrap each burger with 2 bacon slices, securing in place with a wooden cocktail stick.

3 Heat a heavy-based frying pan and add the oil. When hot, add the burgers and cook over medium heat for 5–6 minutes on each side, or until thoroughly cooked through. Serve the burgers at once.

4 Serve the burgers immediately in crusty rolls on a bed of lettuce and red onion rings and topped with mayonnaise and spring onions.

chicken fajitas

ingredients

SERVES 4

3 tbsp olive oil, plus extra
    for drizzling

3 tbsp maple syrup or honey

1 tbsp red wine vinegar

2 garlic cloves, crushed

2 tsp dried oregano

1–2 tsp dried
    red pepper flakes

salt and pepper

4 skinless, boneless
    chicken breasts

2 red peppers, deseeded and
    cut into 2.5-cm/1-inch
    strips

8 flour tortillas, warmed

method

1 Place the oil, maple syrup, vinegar, garlic, oregano, pepper flakes, salt and pepper in a large, shallow plate or bowl and mix together.

2 Slice the chicken across the grain into slices 2.5 cm/1 inch thick. Toss in the marinade until well coated. Cover and chill in the refrigerator for 2–3 hours, turning occasionally.

3 Heat a griddle pan until hot. Lift the chicken slices from the marinade with a slotted spoon, lay on the griddle pan and cook over medium–high heat for 3–4 minutes on each side, or until cooked through. Remove the chicken to a warmed serving plate and keep warm.

4 Add the peppers, skin-side down, to the griddle pan and cook for 2 minutes on each side. Transfer to the serving plate.

5 Serve at once with the warmed tortillas to be used as wraps.

filo chicken pie

ingredients

SERVES 6–8

1.5 kg/3 lb 5 oz whole
    chicken

1 small onion, halved,
    and 3 large onions,
    chopped finely

1 carrot, sliced thickly

1 celery stalk, sliced thickly

pared rind of 1 lemon

1 bay leaf

10 peppercorns

155 g/5$\frac{1}{2}$ oz butter

55 g/2 oz plain flour

150 ml/5 fl oz milk

salt and pepper

25 g/1 oz kefalotiri or romano
    cheese, grated

3 eggs, beaten

225 g/8 oz filo pastry (work
    with one sheet at a time
    and keep the remaining
    sheets covered with a
    damp tea towel)

method

1 Put the chicken in a large saucepan with the halved onion, carrot, celery, lemon rind, bay leaf and peppercorns. Add cold water to cover and bring to the boil. Cover and simmer for about 1 hour, or until the chicken is cooked.

2 Remove the chicken and set aside to cool. Bring the stock to the boil and boil until reduced to about 625 ml/20 fl oz. Strain and reserve the stock. Cut the cooled chicken into bite-size pieces, discarding the skin and bones.

3 Fry the chopped onions until softened in 55 g/2 oz of the butter. Add the flour and cook gently, stirring, for 1–2 minutes. Gradually stir in the reserved stock and the milk. Bring to the boil, stirring constantly, then simmer for 1–2 minutes until thick and smooth. Remove from the heat, add the chicken and season. Let cool, then stir in the cheese and eggs.

4 Melt the remaining butter and use a little to grease a deep 30 x 20-cm/12 x 8-inch metal baking pan. Cut the pastry sheets in half widthways. Line the pan with one sheet of pastry and brush it with a little melted butter. Repeat with half of the pastry sheets. Spread the filling over the pastry, then top with the remaining pastry sheets, brushing each with butter and tucking down the edges. Bake in a preheated oven, 190°C/375°F/Gas Mark 5, for about 50 minutes, until golden. Serve warm.

chicken kebabs with yogurt sauce

ingredients

SERVES 4

300 ml/10 fl oz Greek-style yogurt

2 garlic cloves, crushed

juice of $1/2$ lemon

1 tbsp chopped fresh herbs such as oregano, dill, tarragon or parsley

salt and pepper

4 large skinned, boned chicken breasts

oil, for oiling

8 firm stems of fresh rosemary, optional

shredded romaine lettuce, to serve

rice, to serve

lemon wedges, to garnish

method

1 To make the sauce, put the yogurt, garlic, lemon juice, herbs, salt and pepper in a large bowl and mix well together.

2 Cut the chicken breasts into chunks measuring about 4 cm/$11/2$ inches square. Add to the yogurt mixture and toss well together until the chicken pieces are coated. Cover and marinate in the refrigerator for about 1 hour. If you are using wooden skewers, soak them in cold water for 30 minutes before use.

3 Preheat the grill. Thread the pieces of chicken onto 8 flat, oiled, metal kebab skewers, wooden skewers or rosemary stems and place on an oiled griddle pan.

4 Cook the kebabs under the grill for about 15 minutes, turning and basting with the remaining marinade occasionally, until lightly browned and tender.

5 Pour the remaining marinade into a saucepan and heat gently but do not boil. Serve the kebabs with shredded lettuce on a bed of rice and garnish with lemon wedges. Accompany with the yogurt sauce.

gingered chicken kebabs

ingredients

SERVES 4

3 skinless, boneless chicken
breasts, cut into small
cubes

juice of 1 lime

2.5-cm/1-inch piece root
ginger, peeled and
chopped

1 fresh red chilli, deseeded
and sliced

2 tbsp vegetable or peanut oil

1 onion, sliced

2 garlic cloves, chopped

1 aubergine, cut into chunks

2 courgettes, cut into thick
slices

1 red pepper, deseeded and
cut into squares

2 tbsp red curry paste

2 tbsp Thai soy sauce

1 tsp jaggery or soft light
brown sugar

boiled rice, with chopped
coriander, to serve

method

1 Put the chicken cubes in a shallow dish. Mix the lime, ginger and chilli together and pour over the chicken pieces. Stir gently to coat. Cover and chill in the refrigerator for at least 3 hours to marinate.

2 Soak 8–12 wooden skewers in cold water for 30 minutes before use, to prevent burning.

3 Thread the chicken pieces onto the soaked wooden skewers and cook under a hot grill for 3–4 minutes, turning frequently, until they are cooked through.

4 Meanwhile, heat the oil in a wok or large frying pan and sauté the onion and garlic for 1–2 minutes, until softened, but not browned. Add the aubergine, courgettes and pepper and cook for 3–4 minutes, until cooked but still firm. Add the curry paste, soy sauce and sugar and cook for 1 minute.

5 Serve hot with boiled rice, stirred through with chopped coriander.

thai-style chicken chunks

ingredients

SERVES 4

4 skinless, boneless chicken
    breasts, cut into small
    chunks

freshly cooked jasmine rice,
    to serve

chopped fresh coriander,
    to garnish

marinade

1 red chilli and 1 green chilli,
    deseeded and finely
    chopped

2 garlic cloves, chopped

50 g/1^3/$_4$ oz chopped fresh
    coriander

1 tbsp finely chopped fresh
    lemon grass

^{1}/$_2$ tsp ground turmeric

^{1}/$_2$ tsp garam masala

2 tsp brown sugar

2 tbsp Thai fish sauce

1 tbsp lime juice

salt and pepper

method

1 To make the marinade, put the red and green chillies, garlic, coriander and lemon grass into a food processor and process until coarsely chopped. Add the turmeric, garam masala, sugar, fish sauce and lime juice, season to taste with salt and pepper and blend until smooth.

2 Put the chicken chunks into a non-metallic (glass or ceramic) bowl, which will not react with acid. Pour over enough marinade to cover the chicken, then cover with clingfilm and chill for at least 2^1/$_2$ hours. Cover the remaining marinade with clingfilm and chill until the chicken is ready.

3 When the chicken chunks are thoroughly marinated, lift them out and barbecue them over hot coals for 20 minutes, or until cooked right through, turning them frequently and basting with the remaining marinade. Arrange the chicken on serving plates with some freshly cooked jasmine rice. Garnish with chopped fresh coriander and serve.

grilled chicken with lemon

ingredients

SERVES 4

4 chicken quarters

grated rind and juice of
    2 lemons

4 tbsp olive oil

2 garlic cloves, crushed

2 sprigs fresh thyme, plus
    extra to garnish

salt and pepper

method

1 Prick the skin of the chicken quarters all over with a fork. Put the chicken pieces in a dish, add the lemon juice, oil, garlic, thyme, salt and pepper, and mix well. Cover and marinate in the refrigerator for at least 2 hours.

2 To cook the chicken, preheat the barbecue or grill. Put the chicken on the barbecue rack or in a griddle pan and baste with the marinade. Cook for 30–40 minutes, basting and turning occasionally, until the chicken is tender. (To test if the chicken is cooked, pierce the thickest part of the chicken pieces with a skewer. If the juices run clear, it is ready.) Serve hot, garnished with thyme sprigs and the grated lemon rind.

traditional roast chicken

ingredients

SERVES 4

25 g/1 oz butter, softened

1 garlic clove,
   finely chopped

3 tbsp finely chopped
   toasted walnuts

1 tbsp chopped
   fresh parsley

salt and pepper

1 oven-ready chicken,
   weighing 1.8 kg/4 lb

1 lime, cut into quarters

2 tbsp vegetable oil

1 tbsp cornflour

2 tbsp water

lime wedges and fresh
   rosemary sprigs,
   to garnish

roast potatoes and a selection
   of freshly cooked
   vegetables, to serve

method

1 Mix 1 tablespoon of the butter with the garlic, walnuts and parsley in a small bowl. Season well with salt and pepper. Loosen the skin from the breast of the chicken without breaking it. Spread the butter mixture evenly between the skin and breast meat. Place the lime quarters inside the body cavity.

2 Pour the oil into a roasting pan. Transfer the chicken to the pan and dot the skin with the remaining butter. Roast in a preheated oven, 190°C/375°F/Gas Mark 5, for 1$3/4$ hours, basting occasionally, until the chicken is tender and the juices run clear when a skewer is inserted into the thickest part of the meat. Lift out the chicken and place on a serving platter to rest for 10 minutes.

3 Blend the cornflour with the water, then stir into the juices in the pan. Stir over low heat until thickened, adding more water if necessary. Garnish the chicken with lime wedges and rosemary sprigs. Serve with roast potatoes and a selection of freshly cooked vegetables and spoon over the thickened juices.

tuscan chicken

ingredients

SERVES 4

2 tbsp plain flour

salt and pepper

4 skinned chicken quarters
    or portions

3 tbsp olive oil

1 red onion, chopped

2 garlic cloves, chopped finely

1 red pepper, deseeded and
    chopped

pinch of saffron threads

150 ml/5 fl oz chicken stock
    or a mixture of chicken
    stock and dry white wine

400 g/14 oz canned
    tomatoes, chopped

4 sun-dried tomatoes in oil,
    drained and chopped

225 g/8 oz portobello
    mushrooms, sliced

115 g/4 oz black olives, pitted

4 tbsp lemon juice

fresh basil leaves, to garnish

tagliatelle, fettuccine or
    tagliarini and crusty bread,
    to serve

method

1 Place the flour on a shallow plate and season with salt and pepper. Coat the chicken in the seasoned flour, shaking off any excess. Heat the olive oil in a large, flameproof casserole. Add the chicken and cook over medium heat, turning frequently, for 5–7 minutes, until golden brown. Remove from the casserole and set aside.

2 Add the onion, garlic and red pepper to the casserole, reduce the heat and cook, stirring occasionally, for 5 minutes, until softened. Meanwhile, stir the saffron into the stock.

3 Stir the tomatoes, with the juice from the can, and the sun-dried tomatoes, mushrooms and olives into the casserole and cook, stirring occasionally, for 3 minutes. Pour in the stock and saffron mixture and the lemon juice. Bring to the boil, then return the chicken to the casserole.

4 Cover and cook in a preheated oven, 180°C/350°F/Gas Mark 4, for 1 hour, until the chicken is tender. Garnish with the basil leaves and serve immediately with pasta and crusty bread.

chicken kiev

ingredients

SERVES 4

4 tbsp butter, softened

1 garlic clove, finely chopped

1 tbsp finely chopped fresh
    parsley

1 tbsp finely chopped fresh
    oregano

salt and pepper

4 skinless, boneless chicken
    breasts

85 g/3 oz fresh white or
    wholemeal breadcrumbs

3 tbsp freshly grated
    Parmesan cheese

1 egg, beaten

250 ml/9 fl oz vegetable oil,
    for deep-frying

slices of lemon and flat-leaf
    parsley sprigs, to garnish

freshly cooked new potatoes
    and selection of cooked
    vegetables, to serve

method

1 Place the butter and garlic in a bowl and mix together well. Stir in the chopped herbs and season well with salt and pepper. Pound the chicken breasts to flatten them to an even thickness, then place a tablespoon of herb butter in the centre of each one. Fold in the sides to enclose the butter, then secure with wooden cocktail sticks.

2 Combine the breadcrumbs and grated Parmesan on a plate. Dip the chicken parcels into the beaten egg, then coat in the breadcrumb mixture. Transfer to a plate, cover and chill for 30 minutes. Remove from the refrigerator and coat in the egg and then the breadcrumb mixture for a second time.

3 Pour the oil into a deep-fryer to a depth that will cover the chicken parcels. Heat until it reaches 180–190°C/350–375°F, or until a cube of bread browns in 30 seconds. Transfer the chicken to the hot oil and deep-fry for 5 minutes, or until cooked through. Lift out the chicken and drain on kitchen paper.

4 Divide the chicken between 4 serving plates, garnish with lemon slices and parsley sprigs and serve with new potatoes and a selection of vegetables.

chicken fricassée

ingredients

SERVES 4

1 tbsp plain flour

salt and white pepper

4 skinless, boneless chicken
   breasts, about 140 g/5 oz
   each, trimmed of all visible
   fat and cut into 2-cm/
   ³/₄-inch cubes

1 tbsp sunflower or corn oil

8 pearl onions

2 garlic cloves, crushed

250 ml/8 fl oz chicken stock

2 carrots, diced

2 celery stalks, diced

225 g/8 oz frozen peas

1 yellow pepper, deseeded
   and diced

115 g/4 oz white mushrooms,
   sliced

125 ml/4 fl oz low-fat plain
   yogurt

3 tbsp chopped fresh parsley

method

1 Spread out the flour on a dish and season with salt and pepper. Add the chicken and, using your hands, coat in the flour. Heat the oil in a heavy-based saucepan. Add the onions and garlic and cook over low heat, stirring occasionally, for 5 minutes. Add the chicken and cook, stirring, for 10 minutes, or until just beginning to colour.

2 Gradually stir in the stock, then add the carrots, celery and peas. Bring to the boil, then reduce the heat, cover and simmer for 5 minutes. Add the pepper and mushrooms, cover and simmer for a further 10 minutes.

3 Stir in the yogurt and chopped parsley and season with salt and pepper. Cook for 1–2 minutes, or until heated through, then transfer to 4 large, warmed serving plates and serve immediately.

pasta & chicken medley

ingredients

SERVES 2

125–150 g/4$\frac{1}{2}$–5$\frac{1}{2}$ oz dried
    pasta shapes, such
    as fusilli

2 tbsp mayonnaise

2 tsp bottled pesto sauce

1 tbsp sour cream

salt and pepper

175 g/6 oz cooked skinless,
    boneless chicken

1–2 celery stalks

1 large carrot

125 g/4$\frac{1}{2}$ oz black grapes
    (preferably seedless)

celery leaves, to garnish

french dressing

1 tbsp wine vinegar

3 tbsp extra virgin olive oil

salt and pepper

method

1 To make the french dressing, whisk all the ingredients together in a jug until smooth.

2 Bring a large, heavy-based saucepan of lightly salted water to the boil. Add the pasta, return to the boil and cook for 8–10 minutes, or until just tender but still firm to the bite. Drain thoroughly, rinse and drain again. Transfer to a bowl and mix in 1 tablespoon of the French dressing while hot. Let stand until cold.

3 Mix the mayonnaise, pesto sauce and sour cream together in a bowl, and season with salt and pepper. Cut the chicken into narrow strips. Cut the celery diagonally into narrow slices. Reserve a few grapes for the garnish, halve the rest and remove any pips. Cut the carrot into julienne strips.

4 Add the chicken, celery, carrot, the halved grapes and the mayonnaise mixture to the pasta and toss thoroughly. Taste and adjust the seasoning, if necessary. Arrange the pasta mixture in 2 serving dishes and garnish with the reserved black grapes and the celery leaves.

chicken lasagne

ingredients

SERVES 6

2 tbsp olive oil

900 g/2 lb fresh ground
   chicken

1 garlic clove, finely chopped

4 carrots, chopped

4 leeks, sliced

500 ml/16 fl oz chicken stock

2 tbsp tomato purée

salt and pepper

115 g/4 oz Cheddar cheese,
   grated

1 tsp Dijon mustard

625 ml/20 fl oz hot béchamel
   sauce (see below)

115 g/4 oz dried no-precook
   lasagne sheets

béchamel sauce

625 ml/20 fl oz milk

1 bay leaf

6 black peppercorns

2 slices of onion

mace blade

4 tbsp butter

6 tbsp plain flour

salt and pepper

wild rocket and Parmesan
   shavings, to serve

method

1 To make the béchamel sauce, pour the milk into a saucepan and add the bay leaf, peppercorns, onion and mace. Heat gently to just below boiling point, then remove from the heat, cover, infuse for 10 minutes, then strain. Melt the butter in a separate saucepan. Sprinkle in the flour and cook over low heat, stirring constantly, for 1 minute. Gradually stir in the milk, then bring to the boil and cook, stirring, until thickened and smooth. Season.

2 Heat the oil in a heavy-based saucepan. Add the chicken and cook over medium heat, breaking it up with a wooden spoon, for 5 minutes, or until browned all over. Add the garlic, carrots and leeks, and cook, stirring occasionally, for 5 minutes. Stir in the chicken stock and tomato purée and season with salt and pepper. Bring to the boil, reduce the heat, cover and simmer for 30 minutes.

3 Whisk half the Cheddar cheese and the mustard into the hot béchamel sauce. In a large ovenproof dish, make alternate layers of the chicken mixture, lasagne and cheese sauce, ending with a layer of cheese sauce. Sprinkle with the remaining Cheddar cheese and bake in a preheated oven, 190°C/375°F/ Gas Mark 5, for 1 hour, or until golden brown and bubbling. Serve immediately, with rocket and Parmesan shavings.

spanish rice with chicken

ingredients

SERVES 4

3 tbsp olive oil

1.25 kg/2 lb 12 oz chicken
   pieces

salt and pepper

2 onions, sliced

175 g/6 oz long-grain rice

125 ml/4 fl oz dry white wine

pinch of saffron threads,
   lightly crushed

375 ml/12 fl oz chicken stock

1–2 mild fresh green chillies,
   such as serrano

2 garlic cloves, finely
   chopped

2 beefsteak tomatoes, peeled,
   deseeded and chopped

fresh coriander sprigs,
   to garnish

method

1 Heat 2 tablespoons of the oil in a flameproof casserole. Season the chicken with salt and pepper, add to the casserole and cook over medium heat, turning occasionally, for 8–10 minutes, or until golden. Transfer to a plate with a perforated spoon.

2 Add the remaining oil to the casserole. Add the onions and cook over low heat, stirring occasionally, for 5 minutes, or until translucent. Add the rice and cook, stirring, for 2 minutes, or until the grains are transparent and coated with oil.

3 Pour in the wine. Bring to the boil, then reduce the heat, cover and simmer for 8 minutes, or until all the liquid has been absorbed. Combine the saffron and stock and pour into the casserole. Stir in the chillies and garlic and season with salt. Cover and simmer for 15 minutes.

4 Add the tomatoes and return the chicken pieces to the casserole, pushing them down into the rice. Cover and cook for a further 25 minutes, or until the chicken is cooked through and tender. Garnish with coriander sprigs and serve.

This edition published by Parragon in 2008

Parragon
Queen Street House
4 Queen Street
Bath BA1 1HE, UK

Copyright © Parragon Books Ltd 2007

ISBN 978-1-4075-3087-1

Printed in China

Notes for the reader
• This book uses both metric and imperial measurements. Follow the same units of measurement throughout; do not mix metric and imperial. All spoon measurements are level: teaspoons are assumed to be 5 ml, and tablespoons are assumed to be 15 ml. Unless otherwise stated, milk is assumed to be full fat, eggs and individual vegetables are medium, and pepper is freshly ground black pepper.
• The times given are an approximate guide only. Preparation times differ according to the techniques used by different people and the cooking times may also vary from those given. Optional ingredients, variations or serving suggestions have not been included in the calculations.
• Recipes using raw or very lightly cooked eggs should be avoided by infants, the elderly, pregnant women, convalescents and anyone suffering from an illness. Pregnant and breastfeeding women are advised to avoid eating peanuts and peanut products. Sufferers from nut allergies should be aware that some of the ready-made ingredients used in the recipes in this book may contain nuts. Always check the packaging before use.